anythink

D0768829

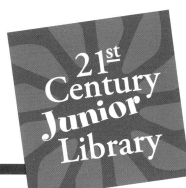

21st Century Junior Library

# Eat a Balanced Diet!

*by Katie Marsico*

CHERRY LAKE PUBLISHING * ANN ARBOR, MICHIGAN

Published in the United States of America by Cherry Lake Publishing
Ann Arbor, Michigan
www.cherrylakepublishing.com

Content Adviser: Kevin Allen, NASM - CPT, Metabolic Technician, Life Time Fitness, Novi, MI

Reading Adviser: Marla Conn, ReadAbility, Inc

Photo Credits: © MilicaStankovic/Thinkstock Photos, cover; © Tatyana Vyc/Shutterstock Images, 4;
© Yurkina Alexandra/Shutterstock Images, 6; © AntonioDiaz/Shutterstock Images, 8; © Amnarj
Tanongrattana/Shutterstock Images, 10; © CandyBox Images/Shutterstock Images, 12; © Arina P
Habich/Shutterstock Images, 14; © R.Ashrafov/Shutterstock Images, 16; © mama_mia/
Shutterstock Images, 18; © alexskopje/Shutterstock Images, 20

**LIBRARY OF CONGRESS CATALOGING-IN-PUBLICATION DATA**
Marsico, Katie, 1980-
  Eat a balanced diet!/By Katie Marsico.
      pages cm.—(Your healthy body.)
  Includes index.
  Audience: 6-10
  Audience: K to grade 3
  ISBN 978-1-63188-983-7 (hardcover)—ISBN 978-1-63362-061-2 (pdf)—
ISBN 978-1-63362-022-3 (pbk.)—ISBN 978-1-63362-100-8 (ebook)
  1.  Nutrition—Juvenile literature. I. Title.
RA784.M3614 2015
613.2—dc23                                          2014021520

*Cherry Lake Publishing would like to acknowledge the work of*
*The Partnership for 21st Century Skills.*
*Please visit* www.p21.org *for more information.*

Printed in the United States of America
Corporate Graphics

# CONTENTS

Fruit makes a smart addition to a healthy meal.

# Let's Talk About Lunch!

**W**hat's growling? It's Jada's stomach! She's hungry for lunch. Jada stares into the refrigerator. So many choices! What foods should she put on her plate?

**Think!** Think about everything you ate yesterday. What did you have for breakfast, lunch, and dinner? How about snacks and desserts? Why did you choose these foods?

5

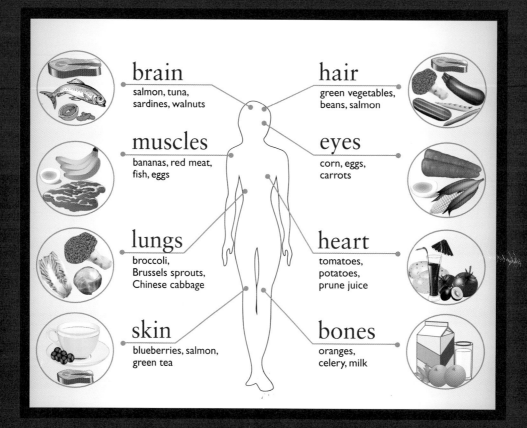

brain
salmon, tuna, sardines, walnuts

hair
green vegetables, beans, salmon

muscles
bananas, red meat, fish, eggs

eyes
corn, eggs, carrots

lungs
broccoli, Brussels sprouts, Chinese cabbage

heart
tomatoes, potatoes, prune juice

skin
blueberries, salmon, green tea

bones
oranges, celery, milk

Eating a variety of foods helps your whole body.

Luckily, Jada's dad offers to help. They'll make a meal that is both tasty *and* **nutritious**! Lunchtime is the perfect time to talk about eating a balanced diet. It's based on eating the right types and amounts of certain foods. Your body needs these foods to grow and stay healthy.

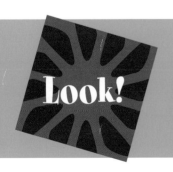

**Look!**

Take a look at this diagram. Which of these foods do you eat regularly? Which of them should you eat more often? How do your favorite foods help you grow?

Milk and milk products keep your teeth and bones strong and healthy.

**Nutritionists** and **dietitians** study which amounts of each food group form a balanced diet. A balanced diet features all the food groups, spread throughout breakfast, lunch, dinner, and a snack. The groups are fruits, vegetables, grain, protein, and **dairy**.

**Make a Guess!**

Some people aren't able to **digest** dairy products. Guess what they pour on their cereal instead of cows' milk. Hint: Many stores sell milk and milk products made from other foods. They include **soy**, almonds, hazelnuts, oats, rice, and coconut!

Fruits and vegetables are full of different vitamins that your body needs.

# Helping Build a Healthy Body

Jada searches for all the different food groups in her kitchen. Some of the first foods she finds are broccoli, carrots, corn, and onions. She spots apples, strawberries, blueberries, and cantaloupe as well.

Jada's dad explains that vegetables and fruits contain **nutrients**. They help keep a person's heart, blood, eyes, skin, and

Breads with natural and multiple grains have more nutrients than white bread.

teeth healthy. These nutrients also support digestion and **immunity**.

Grain products include rice, pasta, bread, and cereal. They help a person's body break down food into energy. The nutrients in protein foods are used to create **tissue** and blood cells. **Poultry**, beef, and seafood are protein foods. So are eggs, nuts, beans, and peas.

Dairy products include milk, cheese, and yogurt. They help build healthy bones and teeth.

Helping in the kitchen is a good way to learn more about food.

The oils found in nuts, vegetables, and fish contain nutrients, too. They support skin and eye health. They also strengthen a person's immune and nervous systems. But oils aren't an official food group. They are a form of fat. They should be eaten only in small amounts, but not avoided completely. Our bodies burn fat as a way to get energy.

With the right meat and vegetables, stir-fry is just one example of a tasty, healthy meal!

# Making the Perfect Meal

Jada and her dad gather items from each food group. At last, it's time to make lunch.

First, Dad chops up an onion, broccoli, peppers, and chicken. He cooks them in a pan on the stove top. Meanwhile, he boils a package of whole-grain pasta. Then Jada mixes the pasta with the vegetables and chicken.

Putting berries on frozen yogurt is a good way to add some vitamins to your dessert.

Only a few more food groups to go.
Jada knows Dad loves frozen yogurt.
And Jada knows their balanced lunch is
missing a dairy product. For a topping,
Dad suggests they use fresh berries. It's the
perfect end to a perfect meal!

After lunch, Jada and her dad clean
up. Then they decide to walk to the store.
Walking is good exercise. Exercise helps
build a healthy body, too.

Check your grocery list to be sure your family is buying items from each food group!

Plus, Jada and Dad have to buy more groceries. They are thinking about what foods they will need to make a delicious, nutritious dinner!

**Create!**

Create a meal plan for the week ahead. Talk to your family, and write down the foods you'll use every day. Be sure to include items from each food group! Remind your family to review the plan before they shop for groceries or cook.

# GLOSSARY

**dairy** (DER-ee) foods or drinks made from milk produced by mammals such as cows

**dietitians** (dye-uh-TIH-shuhnz) workers whose job involves giving people advice about how to eat a healthy diet

**digest** (dye-JEST) to use body parts and processes to break down food into nutrients and waste

**immunity** (ih-MYOO-ni-tee) the body's ability to fight off infections and diseases

**nutrients** (NU-tree-uhnts) substances that living things need to grow and stay healthy

**nutritionists** (nu-TRIH-shuh-nists) workers whose job involves giving people advice about how food affects health

**nutritious** (nu-TRIH-shuhss) containing substances that living things need to grow and stay healthy

**poultry** (POLE-tree) farm birds, such as chickens and turkeys, that are raised for their meat or eggs

**soy** (SOI) soybeans and food products made from soybeans

**tissue** (TIH-shoo) material that forms certain body parts in people and animals

# FIND OUT MORE

## BOOKS

Borgert-Spaniol, Megan. *Vegetable Group*. Minneapolis: Bellwether Media, 2012.

Clark, Katie. *Balanced Meals*. Mankato, MN: The Child's World, 2013.

Fromer, Liza, Francine Gerstein, and Joe Weissmann (illustrator). *My Healthy Body*. Toronto: Tundra Books, 2012.

## WEB SITES

### Health Canada—Eating Well with Canada's Food Guide
*http://www.hc-sc.gc.ca/fn-an /food-guide-aliment/index-eng.php* Check out a more detailed version of the guide Canadians use to follow a balanced diet.

### United States Department of Agriculture (USDA)— MyPlate Kids' Place
*www.choosemyplate.gov/KIDS* Enjoy games, videos, songs, and recipes that provide more information on healthy eating and balanced meals.

# INDEX

## ABOUT THE AUTHOR

Katie Marsico is the author of more than 150 children's books. She lives in a suburb of Chicago, Illinois, with her husband and children.